Dedicated To:
Dan & Olivia Rose

itten By: Abigail Gartland

Hello, my name is St. Rose!

I was born in Lima, Peru in 1586!

When I was born my parents named me Isabel, but as I grew up, I was so beautiful that everyone called me Rose!

After I was confirmed in the church, I made Rose my official name

From the time I was only a little girl, I knew I wanted to be a nun.

I went to Mass every single day to receive Jesus in the Eucharist

At night, I would only sleep for two hours, so I could pray and pray.

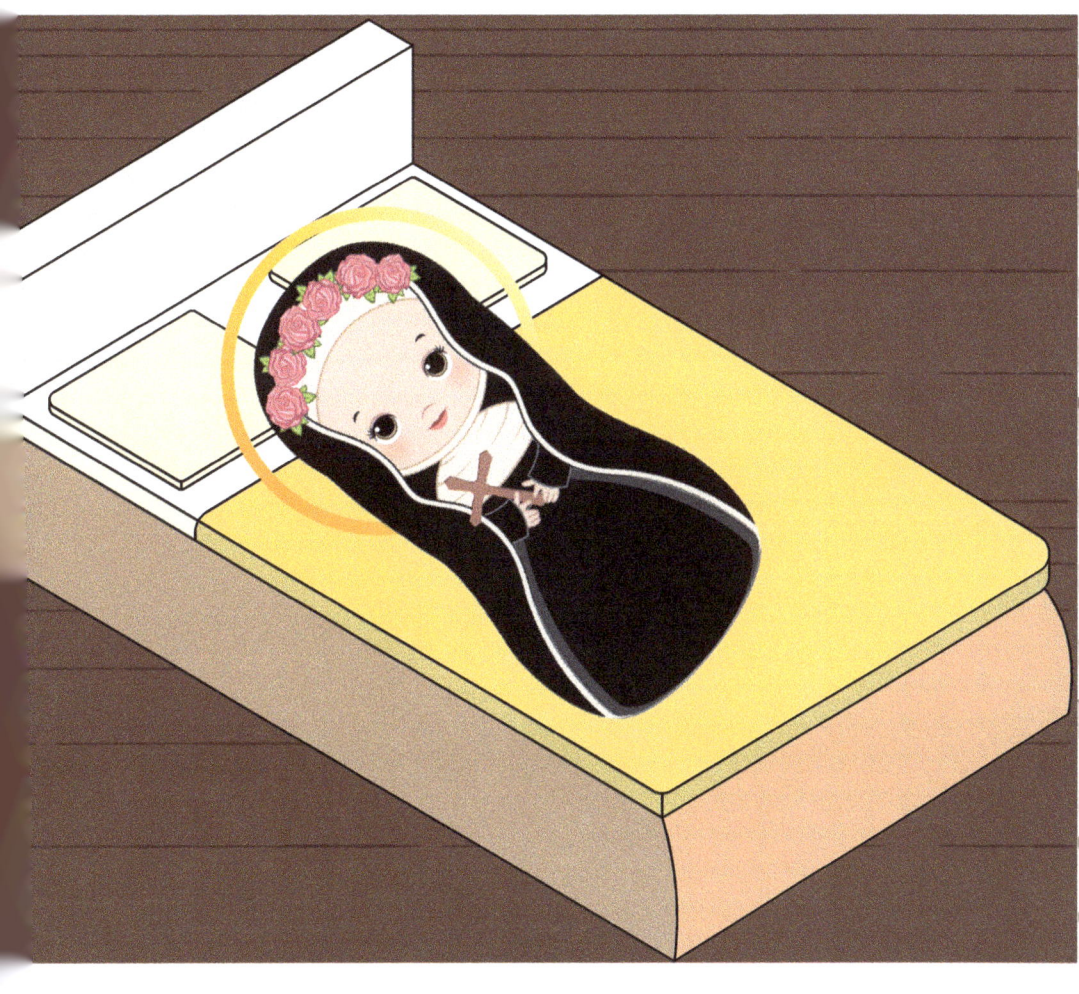

I loved spending all of my time with Jesus!

In August of 1617, Jesus called me to come to Him in Heaven.

Do you want to be more like me?

You can celebrate my feast day with me on August 23rd.

I am the patron saint of the Philippines and Latin America!

I pray for you every day of your life.

St. Rose of Lima

Pray for us!

About the Author

Abigail Gartland

I love the saints and I love my faith. The idea for sharing the stories of the saints with little ones came when my dear friends were expecting their first baby. I wanted to create something as unique and special as our friendship. Each book is dedicated to very special people and groups who have enriched my faith in different ways. I am blessed to write these stories and appreciate the unending support of my family and friends. When I am not writing am a middle school teacher. I hope you enjoy these stories. I pray for each and every person who opens one of my books to learn more about the saints.

Abbie

www.ingramcontent.com/pod-product-compliance
Lightning Source LLC
LaVergne TN
LVHW061634070526
838199LV00071B/6667